Jim Erasmus Lime Templeton

JELHEAD

By Jim Templeton

Edited by Russell Payne

ISBN 978-1-4478-8421-7

J
E
L
H
E
A
D

Jim Templeton's poetry is in a constant fluid state, he has been known to change all but the title of a poem at some performances, insisting that he is inspired as much by his surroundings and audience as he is by any sequential language he may have prepared earlier. So these poems are a mix of transcripts from various bootleg recordings of performances in the eighties and nineties, and a few more recent readings in London and New York.

Jim famously refuses to write down his verse. In 1999, a napkin used by him to write down the first few verses of "Nahuatl Toroid" sold on Ebay.Com for over £200. Rumour has it that the napkin was bought by the late Marlon Brando who promptly burned the napkin "to preserve the myth".

-Russell Payne

With thanks to J.Osbourne, Kim Telier, Mad Francis, A.Pacino and Dr Jacob Bernstein for their contributions.

Contents-

ANSWERHORN

Listen
Listen
Listen to the answers
to all of the questions
to which of the questions?
to ALL of the questions
but which are the questions?
All of the questions

The answerhorn
It's talking to me
The answerhorn
First answer is free
The answerhorn

Listen.....

To
thousands of very quick random
words
No no!
Not now!
I missed what it said.
Was it yes
or did the answerhorn
tell me what I don't want to hear?

Break it
crush the answerhorn
make it silent before it tells me
the truth

The answerhorn
It's talking to me
The answerhorn
First answer is free
The answerhorn
Tell me
Tell me
tell me

#

Woooooooooohoooooooooooooooooooooooo!

I'm sorry. I don't have anybody to physically do it here.

COLD YOU COLD

Your face is all blistered
all red and horrible
oh no, oh no, oh nonono

Ha ha, I remember when you
were so normal
it wasn't so much the way you
looked oh yeah
leaning over the table
I tried not to stare
but I did
soft as
soft as
soft as.....

I type the reply for most of the morning
I'm sorry I just don't want you anymore
your face is all blistered and red
It's like leprosy or something
you say it's just fake tan gone wrong
I know it must be something far worse
like that thing
the singing
detective was bringing
with him before he died of it.

Your hair is all patchy too
I used to like that but not
anymore
What am I up to now?
I'm getting as far away
as I possibly can.
Support you in your needy hour?

No, thanks
I can't look at those blisters.

I'll Come back when you get better.

Write me.

DIFFERENT EXAMPLE

Wheezing electronic dissapointment
fake samples of a hollow ancient joke
the nasal hardly heard announcments
frothing out the words that you just spoke

Yellow empty rings on the agenda
I'd like to add, or if I might could just
it never means anything meaning slender
until the edges are all left to rust

This isn't making sense to me now either
It's just like one more comparative noun
and when I think you were a true beleiver
how does it make me feel? It gets me down.

I need to find a different example
to illustate to you just how I feel

FAMOUS AVOIDING

There's a library full of well-known books
I haven't read a word of
A ton of famous people
I've never even heard of

A world of hurt
A life of pain
I've never had to suffer
A wife I've never had
can't ever leave me
for another

LIFE GARAGE

At the back

No, not there! At the back

behind the screwdrivers and the stuffed animals,
behind the motorbike engine and the lawnmowers,
behind the cool chrome bumpers and rabbit hutch

there it is, over there, at the back, mind the rust.

It's my life.

All wrapped up in old soiled sheets and duct taped together
damp patches and rust patches and mould patches
should've looked after it better.

It's my life.

Someone must have run a lawnmower into the side of it,
It's not gonna work anymore, but don;t throw it out
it just might come in useful someday, to someone,
but no, I don't want it

It's broken.

GREAT MISTAKES

Trusting Mr Wily Fox
Opening Pandora's box

Trusting Mr Wily Fox
Opening Pandora's box

Trusting Mr Wily Fox
Opening Pandora's box

Trusting Mr Wily Fox
Opening Pandora's box

Trusting Mr Wily Fox
Opening Pandora's box

Trusting a Pandoras Fox
Open Mr Wily's box

Trusting a Pandoras Fox
Open Mr Wily's box
Trusting a Pandoras Fox
Open Mr Wily's box

Trusting a Pandoras Fox
Open Mr Wily's box

Trusting a Pandoras Fox
Open Mr Wily's box

Trusting Mr Wily Fox
Opening Pandora's box

Foxing Mr Box
As he opens Pandora's Trust

WIKI

You know you can't avoid me
You worried you annoyed me

give me the satisfaction
of an action
packed in
refracting
back a the acting
the machine

I'm fly on the mike
and try as you like
you can't imitate the great sheik
you flakey fake second-rate
from the great lakes

THE CONSTANT SPECTE OF ABANDONMENT

The constant specte of abandonment

Don't leave me like this
Don't leave me at all

Like a lemsip for the senses
checked it antiseptic hectic life we lead.

VERNOL

Hummingbirds all stranded
in an amber haze of doubt
they cannot pause to smell the breeze
before the breeze runs out

Run down the dimensions
north, up, left, in and now
backwards, thought, inspiration
green, yedellion, splow.

Rock mass and silt land
and nothing for today
the oldest known surviving memory
of last Wednesday.

humming in the background
from the laminator spread
sunlight through the foreground
and into the lens forcefed

ram through the transfer of
my most precious defeat
and walk away from saturday
before there's chance to meet.

worried now the few time can't

divide into the old
and we'll all forget the what
was it you tell me you were told?

Standing on a mountain
wearing nothing but my socks
It not a truth so it must
be the Vernol equinox.

Tell me children

Tell me children

Tell me my bewildered child

Hummingbirds abandoned
in an amber haze of doubt
they cannot pause to smell the breeze
before it all runs out

Run down the dimensions
from eight to forty four
pull the plug and leave me
alone and on the floor

Can't you all see now
how important it all is
forsee the Vernol equinox

and tell me what it means?

BLUE FOOD

Bananas are yellow
Peaches are peach
Apples are red, sometimes green
all sorts of vegetables in green,orange, brown
but there one colour quite rarely seen

blue food
i'd like more
blue food
new tasty
blue food
i want some
blue food
new food
blue food

Alright you've got blueberry
and blue M and M's
and if you leave potatoes long enough
they'll go blue in the end
but ask me we still need more

blue food
give me some
blue food
I want to eat

blue food

all kinds of

blue food

new food

blue food

blue. food.

CLIVE

A cardigan criminal, living in the big pill, marginal original, cardinal official with a honorable initial until the hills come alive.

He's Clive five by five alive in the hive

he's Clive gotta archive to survive alive

he's Clive i've i've i've i've got it!

wicky wick wicky wicky

He's Eight feet tall, night light in his hall, too tight to fall, equal rights for all, so mighty you all like to call the right honorable....

Clive.

Give up your fears for a cup of tears and drop the years before hope disappears.

That's Clive.

Once upon a Clive, he's

Clive.

Insider trading beside the grating, can't hide the hating or slide the ratings.

So low he'll never be a blow to liberty or be too slow to flee or bow to the enemy. Try to set you free. bye bye "Let It Be". That guy on TV reminds you of me when I was 23. Blind and in the sea, behind the gravity of the situations brevity, Clive is gonna help you see that none of you are truly free.

The major player in a cage of layers, with Leo Sayer as a gay soothsayer, Cassius Clay as a fey Lord mayor, the goose that lay the golden prayer and Dr Dre as a Hey Hey Heyer.

He's Clive. Five by five by five by five.

He's Clive.

C - live. Clive.

Fantastically masterful, a masterclass in wonderful, past the holy waterfall, past the only canticle, past the lonely afterthought
and..
straight...
on...
till....
morning.

DOG FOUNTAIN

The emperor's drowning in sunlight today
all the dogs are asleep
on white porceline shade
While I'm fighting to keep my head
above water
You're walking upon it
and I'm getting shorter.

The rainwater journal is approaching full
panic is almost inevitable
so why do these things not seem to bother you?
you're too calm
you're too nice
and I don't think it's true.

The fountain is empty, the puppies asleep
my grass has gone yellow in all of this heat
curve of the poolside is slipping away
wake them up quickly to harden the clay.

The glass and the sand reach up to the sky
as blue and as clear as acacia's eye
Why when I reach for you don't you come near?
you're the only
one who
has anything to fear.

Getting back to the end and I see all I can
the plain of complaints and fire of the hand
paper is burning before I can write
and the fireplace is full of Shantabhai delight

Sugar and snow in cubes and on hills
The dogs still asleep waiting until
the water comes home again, up to your ears
too many years
spent waiting
for someone
to take them home.

Nothing left but the dry dust of yesterday now
a horse born of metals, a crumbling cow
a delicate tapestry soaked with your tears
a staircase down to the playfullness years
I've been waiting too long
I've forgotten what for.

Stop looking at me as if I were not there
Just leave me alone and come over here
I like the way that you don't look like today
Go on, go away and please, please won't you stay?

You're putting me down, should be picking me up
Drink from my mug or I'll misplace your cup

Be on my side or I don't want to play

Sit down over here and please, please go away.

I LOVE HER

Rotten way to tell me
but I think I got the message
You made me a nut salad
and put it in the garbage
I wanted to forgive you
but I was really hungry
and throwing out the leafy greens
really made me angry.

I love her
Even though she threw away my tea
I love her
and I know that she loves me

On tuesday it was garlic bread
and one two three cheese pizza
I came home early from my work
I only wished to please her
The pizza wasn't ready yet
it was still in the freezer
she used it like a frisbee
when I tried to gently tease her.

I love her
Even though she threw away my tea
I love her

and I know that she loves me

Took her to a restaurant
not a cheap one but a nice one
I ordered all three courses
and some biscuits with cheese on
the starter it had just arrived
made a joke about last night
I was covered in italian food
before I got a bite

I love her
Even though she threw away my tea
I love her
and I know
I know that she loves me
I love her
though she always throws my meals
I love her
and I know that it's for real.

LAMPSHADES

Lampshade obscuring my view
the hills of my memory are blue
Return to the true life I knew
before you
before you

I can snap the thoughts cleanly in half
until I just see tiles and the bath
is it not enough to hear your laugh?
are you through?
are you through?

Too many lampshades
too many lampshades
all my lights are now blocked out
Don't make me do this
It's really not too late
We can both look together for the way out
I know there's too much on your plate.
Don't say any more you'll regret
I just hate it
When you do that.
Too many lampshades.

JFOK

I don't remember where I was when Kennedy
was blown away live on TV
Or what I was doing when the twin towers fell
I'm sorry but I just can't tell

But I remember every tiny thing about the moment I met you
I thought to myself "Hey, I won't forget you"
Where we were.
How you wore your hair.
What day it was.
and that's because

I'm in love with you and I don't care about JFK.

It was half past two on a summertime Wednesday.

I'm in love with you and I don't care about JFK.

I know I sometimes forgot to comb my hair
put something down and then forget where.
I can't recall the name of your Uncle Phil
or to pay the electricity bill

I'm late for meetings and early for tea
I keep thinking 2 o'clock is half past three
Can't find the club though I'm a lifetime member.

I've forgotten more things than I remember

I don't know what day it is anymore
I spent an hour a day on the bathroom floor
I need a special machine to make me breathe
and I can't remember what made you leave.

I'm in love with you and I don't care about JFK.

It was half past two on a summertime Wednesday.

I'm in love with you and I don't care about JFK.

THADDEUS BLANK

Feeling full of power
Sitting on the bus
past the water tower
and the terminus

an integrated package of anonymous
into the room comes Thaddeus

Mr Blank wouldn't thank you for turning up
an inviolate redemption from the shoulders up
give him what he wants and them he might give up
knock him down, lock the door before he get's up

Feeling full of power
clinging to the door
you could do with a shower
like never before

Give in to Mr Thaddeus Blank
he won't thank
you

I can see him now,
in racing green
ladling out the omniverse
and juggling the scene

Thad
e-us
Ba
lank

MANLORD CAPABLE.

Looking at the clouds again
Swimming in my head
All but one of the babymen
are feeding in my shed

Understanding the underworld
Living by your ears
Four and twenty parasites
picking at your fear

It's been too long since the last time
I knew another voice
Where's my machine redeemer?
He said I had a choice

A shovel in the roof betrays
the absence of security
they confiscated all my food
"because of the impurity"

We need someone to follow
a slave risen from the ranks
to unlock all the hidden vaults
and open up the banks

A sea of new humanity

a tidal wave of change
we have to listen to all he says
before he's washed away.

Yodel choir of terpitude
jumping on the shops
The ramifications of Felix
the rain that never stops.

He is the trout leader
his voice it commands respect
he's the dream feeder
he always knows whats best
he's the ultimate breeder
he'll make sure the world if full
There's no one greedier
Here is the Manlord Capable.

The booming voice sings
"Kneel before me
 Express your love
 I've come with goodness
 From above"

Inescapable.
Unmistakable.
Cannot wait until.
Come and feel the thrill.

He wants, needs, can and will.

Damned to now fulfil.

Not even on the

Contents page.

Manlord Capable.

WHEN I SING

In the winter of 67 I wrote to Martin Luther King.
Junior.
He had inspired me, I said, to be a singer.
A crooner.
Which might seem odd, what does singing have.
To do.
With Civil Rights and the righteous fight.
Of the few.
To stand up and be counted, like Claudette
And Rosa.
I'll tell you. If it wasn't for Mr King, I wouldn't have
Applied.
If it wasn't for him, I probably would not have.
Tried.
To stand out form the crowd, and not be.
Afraid.
Of the way people saw me or how I was.
Portrayed.
Thanks.
To.
Him.
In the winter of 67 I wrote to Martin Luther King.
Junior.
He never replied, it makes me wish I'd written.
Sooner.
I have left behind my former anxiety.

I'm not afraid of an oppressive authority.

No longer scared of a disapproving majority.

I make openness and justice my personal priorities.

I am proud to be an ethnic minority.

Now when I sing.

I sing for Martin.

SHE LEADS ME

In comparison, I am a child

holding her hand, needing her smile

She just gives, losing health

to myself, my selfish self

A newborn spring, across my way

Surprising like the other day

She leads me to the path I need

To stem the flow and stop the bleed

Killing time that needs to die

She still must stop and wonder why

the only time I support her

is when I have the time to spare.

In comparison, I am a child

Outside the shops, waiting while

she buys a skirt, above the knee

I need her, but she leads me.

TRIANGULAR BOAT

I have a hat that has three sides

And each of those is blue

The one that is not blue but red

Is on the side with you

The red side is the underside

And undecided too

As to if it is the side

That is not red but blue

The only way we can decide

If we can find the truth

Is to deride and vilify

Why my side lied untrue

To try the side that lied beside

the triangular boat

I must evoke a hindsight lie

And see which side can float.

SEVENTEEN PIECES OF SELLOTAPE

The hearse pulls up beside the Mini Metro

In uteri humility can best describe

The feeling that I am feeling this time

Am I the only plant to need water?

Or is it true that the vermillion sprouts

As often as the kissing tree does?

My cat lies out before the flowers of its own making

Rotting before it can escape

The web of great mistakes leads beyond this

But to where?

Thirty Eight, The Road, The Town, The County

AB1 1AB

Mr John Horatio Tiberius Muriel Doe

Bright dreams of the corpse desk

Dead before it lived and alive yet

The sticky yellow sideburns of it

No questions really answered

I liked the sound of it at the time

It sounded nice

Just a hot room and broken promises

Asking whether the service is up to date

We only know our hours and no more besides

Tony bases his life around a guide

That appears to be out of date

And it is because you know why?

Because goodness knows

Once around the block and back again

Goodness knows

Being here doesn't make any difference at all

He doesn't know I'm here

She doesn't know why I'm here

Something like that

But two papers and seventeen pieces of sellotape don't make any sort of plot

They just make it look pretentious

Petty

Balancing between broken and happy

Pretty

An eye thief there only as long as he needs to be

Before he takes all you hold dear

And sells it to strangers.

2012

Twenty Twelve
The space year
Utopia
Everyone happy
Jetpacs and flying cars
Food in pill form
No disease
No war
No more.

I was lied to.

Facebook
Twitter
Youtube
LOL
ROFL
Social networking
Manufactured talent
Manufactured conflicts
Fractured childhoods
Poverty
Disease
Famine
Cellphones
The X Factor

No Jetpacs

It wouldn't be so bad if we at least had
Jetpacs

Sadface

☹

One
Word
Describes
My
Pain
I
Cannot
Write
It
Down
I
Cannot
Say
It
Loud
I
    Can
      Only
        Show
          You
Come see me after life.

TRACTOR NAME SUGGESTIONS-

Doug

Mike Blythe

Roger

Bucephalus

Timmy

Tommy

Terry

Red Thunder

Red Raider

Red Rider

Stinky

Big Bore

Twinkle

Tarquin

The Fabulous Rammstein

Colonel Muriel Volestrangler

La Tractor De Garry

Trudy

Ted

The Triumphant Love Missile

Max Factor (the little red tractor)

Ulysses

Marengo

Snowball

Torque of the town

The Motorvator

Bigdog

Comanche

Hercules

Psycho

Fang

Basil

Mavis

Barbara

Margaret

Floyd

Dougal

Digger

The Red Death

Lightning

Trigger

Champion (the wonder tractor)

Simon

Polly

Scoop

Earth-Hawk, scourge of the French Fields

Mickey

Tony

Plum

Russell

Horace

Weedy

Garry

HIGH DEFINITION

Define how high you can go

As far as What? Who?

Self help means wealth tells us meaning. Eat some ozone.

Your only limitations are the self prescribed attitudes you bring along with yourself that stem from a childhood marked by nothing more than everyone else. We all have it bad, we all have it good, stop thinking that what happens to you is any worse than what happens to him what matters is how you react to the past how much you allow it to define the future.

Every moment, any moment, can be the start of whatever you want it to be. Make it this moment. Stop being such a bleating child and take responsibility for your own outcome.

Your father and mother cannot define how much you love your own children.

Your bank account does not define how happy you are.

Your lovers do not define how much love you are capable of.

Your diet does not define what sort of contribution you will make to society or what dress size you wear or if you will die young.

Your limitations do not define your limits.

Define how high you can go.

Egg nore the signs.

You're wrong.

Go long.

JOLLY

Say that to me again

Just one more time

Just think it

Look at me with those amber

eyes and

Think it

That's all its going to

take

To make me do

something

some

thing

were both going to regret

Stupid

Senseless stressless mess less con fess less stress chess address
compress

Don't point either

Now shut up and be jolly

URGENT NEED OF ATTENTION

Charlie Sheen

Mr Sheen

Eddie Sheen

James Dean

David Cameron

Coconut Cameron

David Cameroon

Camerloon

Too soon.

David Frosty reception

The privation of self

The duvet bombing of truth

Hiding underneath your own shadow

Can you now add David to the list

He turned up late

A blue quality street wrapper worn like a cloak

Hair on fire

Green hands holding plastic markers

Pee Cee Essential

Just leave it

It's not worth it

It's not even funny or clever

To be funny and clever

anymore

ENVELOPED IN THE KIND WARMTH OF DAYTIME TELEVISION

Hours.

Days.

Weeks.

Years.

Phone now.

Don't phone now.

Win a hair removal system

The answer is probably A.

It no longer matters.

The chances of winning

Are astronomical.

Complete this poem

Roses are red

Violets are _____

A) Blue

B) Hippopotomous

C) Mohandas Karamchand Gandhi

Closing date for entries is the 31st October at 5pm

You must be 18 years or over to enter this competition.

Acknowledgements-

Stef Germanotta

Charlie Sheen

Jim Templeton Snr.

Russell Payne

Enrico Fermi

Josephine Baker

David Henderson

J.Osbourne

Kim Telier

F.Rossi

A.Pacino

Dr Jacob Bernstein

J. Depp

JELHEAD

"It's not what you say, it's what you think you say, not even that, it's what they think you think you say, so stop writing this down, there's no point.."